SCAMMERS PARADISE!: An Explosive
Insider Account of Nigeria's Internet Scam
Industry

By Frederick Amakom

DEDICATION

This book is dedicated to the countless innocent men and women across the world who have fallen victim to internet fraud—and to the millions of honest Nigerians whose reputations have been unfairly stained by the crimes of a few.

Published by Frederick Amakom Publishing

Printed in USA

PREFACE — Inside Nigeria's Hidden Scam Economy

For years, millions of internet users across the world have opened their inboxes to find messages promising inheritances, partnerships, love, charity, or emergency assistance—messages that often originate from Nigeria. Many recipients ignore them. Many others, unfortunately, do not.

The losses run into billions of dollars.
The human consequences are immeasurable.

These crimes go by many names: internet scam, advance-fee fraud, email schemes, NGO fraud, romance scam. In Nigeria, one name encompasses all of them—
419.

Behind the headlines and stereotypes is an underground industry that employs thousands of young Nigerians. It operates on secrecy, fear, spiritual oaths, and a powerful code of silence reinforced by religious figures, native doctors, syndicate bosses, and community complicity. Its size has long been underestimated because few have ever penetrated its inner circle.

This book attempts to do what no external investigator could accomplish:
tell the story from the inside, without censorship, without filtering, and without outside interpretation.

Who are the scammers?
Why do they join?
How are they recruited, trained, and protected?
What role do religion and traditional beliefs play?
How do they operate across borders?
And what does the world get wrong about them?

For decades, every attempt to document the 419 underworld has scratched only the surface. Journalists, law-enforcement agents, and academics often encounter a wall of silence.

But Lucas, the narrator of this story, came from within the system.

His journey reveals not only the mechanics of fraud, but the psychological, social, and economic pressures that pull young people into it. His story exposes the real hierarchy, the criminal techniques, the spiritual fears, and the human conflicts within one of Africa's most infamous underground economies.

This is that story—raw, unfiltered, and as close to the truth as the inner circle allows.

INTRODUCTION — Understanding the Reality Behind Nigeria's Scam Industry

For decades, the conversation around Nigerian internet fraud has been dominated by stereotypes, sensational media reports, and shallow commentary. What the world often sees is only the surface: an email from a supposed prince, a romance scam, or a fraudulent investment offer. What people rarely understand is the internal machinery, motivations, pressures, and psychological processes that push thousands of young Nigerians into this underworld.

This book is not fiction. It is not an attempt to glorify crime or repackage it as entertainment. It is a firsthand account of how a young man — raised in a religious home, educated, hopeful, and determined to succeed honestly — became entangled in one of Africa's most infamous criminal industries.

My goal is simple:
To help the world understand *how* this happens, *why* it continues, and *what it looks like from the inside.*

Where journalists often encounter secrecy, denial, or filtered stories, I lived the reality. I interacted with syndicates, spiritual figures, native doctors, and young men who risked everything for quick wealth. I saw the internal hierarchy, the training structures, the psychological conditioning, and the mechanisms used to sustain loyalty and silence.

This book documents that journey — truthfully, directly, and responsibly — so readers, policy makers, researchers, and parents can understand what really happens behind the scenes.

▤ TABLE OF CONTENTS

Scammers Paradise!: An Explosive Insider Account of Nigeria's Internet Scam Industry
By Frederick Amakom

Front Matter

- Title Page
- Dedication
- Preface
- Introduction — *Inside Nigeria's Hidden Scam Economy*

PART I — THE JOURNEY INTO THE UNDERWORLD

Chapter 1 — The Letter That Changed My Direction

Chapter 2 — The Conversation No Child Wants to Have

Chapter 3 — Arriving in a City That Demands Transformation

Chapter 4 — Inside a Lifestyle That Redefines Moral Compass

Chapter 5 — Pressure, Poverty, and the Moment That Broke Me

PART II — RITUALS, RECRUITMENT & PSYCHOLOGICAL CONTROL

Chapter 6 — Crossing a Line I Could Never Uncross

Chapter 7 — The Spiritual Architecture of Nigeria's Fraud Underworld

Chapter 8 — Initiation: The Day I Stopped Being Who I Used to Be

PART III — TRAINING IN THE MECHANICS OF DECEPTION

Chapter 9 — Learning the Rules of a Hidden Economy

Chapter 10 — The Anatomy of an International Fraud Network

Chapter 11 — Inside the Training Ground

Chapter 12 — Learning the Script: How Scammers Are Trained to Think and Speak

Chapter 13 — First Blood: The Call That Changed Everything

Chapter 14 — Becoming the Caller

PART IV — CONSEQUENCES, CONFLICT & THE CRACKING OF IDENTITY

Chapter 15 — The Scam Within the Scammers

Chapter 16 — Law Enforcement, Surveillance, and the Constant Threat of Capture

Chapter 17 — What the World Gets Wrong About 419

Chapter 18 — Hitting the Wall: When the Money Can No Longer Numb You

Chapter 19 — Escaping Without Leaving: The Gray Zone Between Fraud and Freedom

Chapter 20 — Closing the Door Without Making Noise

Chapter 21 — The Cost of Silence

Chapter 22 — Rebuilding From the Ground Up

Chapter 23 — The Reason This Story Must Be Told

Conclusion — The Road Back to Myself

Back Matter

- Acknowledgements
- Glossary of Key Terms
- Appendix A: Psychology of Internet Fraud
- Appendix B: Why Youths Enter the Fraud World
- Appendix C: How Victims Can Protect Themselves
- About the Author

 SCAMMERS' PARADISE

By Frederick Amakom

CHAPTER 1 — THE LETTER THAT Changed My Direction

I was raised in a modest Christian home in southeastern Nigeria. My parents, both devoted to their faith, taught us values centered on honesty, diligence, and moral discipline. I carried those teachings through university, believing that with education, perseverance, and prayer, I would eventually secure a stable life.

Reality proved harsher.

After graduation, I entered a job market defined by scarcity, nepotism, and systemic unemployment. For months, I applied for positions across various sectors. I wrote tests, attended interviews, and waited for calls that never came. The longer this continued, the heavier the burden became — not only financially, but emotionally and socially.

In my community, joblessness is not just an economic condition; it is a quiet form of humiliation. People begin to see you differently. Some avoid eye contact. Others whisper. Your confidence erodes slowly. The pressure to "become something" grows daily.

In the middle of one of those frustrating days, I returned home to find a letter from my childhood friend, John Bosco, who was then living in Lagos. We had grown up together, attended the same schools, worshipped in the same church, and shared almost identical aspirations. But while I struggled, his life had taken a dramatically different turn. Within a year, he had acquired wealth that few young men could explain: luxury cars, real estate, international travel, and a reputation that provoked equal parts admiration and suspicion.

His letter did not contain money — something he occasionally sent to support me. Instead, it contained a stark message that I now recognize as the beginning of my shift in direction. He challenged my persistence in seeking legitimate employment and described my continued job hunt as a waste of time. The tone was blunt, almost confrontational. He urged me to relocate to Lagos immediately, describing it as a city where opportunities existed for those willing to take unconventional paths.

His words unsettled me because they carried a brutal truth. My situation was not improving, and my family depended on me. My widowed mother was stretching herself to support my younger sister's schooling. I was becoming the person I feared most — a burden.

That letter forced me to confront a harsh question:
How long can moral conviction survive in the face of prolonged economic desperation?

By that evening, I realized my options were limited. Lagos represented uncertainty, but remaining at home represented failure. I made the decision to leave. Not because I wanted to chase quick wealth like my friend, but because I felt trapped in a system that offered no pathways forward.

That moment — standing over that letter, contemplating my next move — marked a turning point in my life. I did not know then how deeply Lagos would challenge my beliefs, reshape my identity, or pull me into a world I had spent my entire life condemning.

But I knew one thing with painful clarity:
My life could not continue the way it was.

The journey that followed would reveal an entirely different Nigeria — one that operates behind closed doors, fueled by desperation, global inequalities, spiritual manipulation, and an underground economy more organized than most outsiders can imagine.

This is where that story begins.

CHAPTER 2 — THE CONVERSATION THAT NO CHILD WANTS TO HAVE

Leaving home is rarely easy for any young Nigerian, but leaving under pressure, uncertainty, and quiet desperation is an entirely different experience. Before I could pack my bags for Lagos, I needed to speak to the one person whose opinion carried more weight than anyone else's — my mother.

My mother had three deeply held beliefs that shaped her view of the world:

1. **Lagos corrupts young people.**
   In her eyes, Lagos was a city that swallowed morals and spat out hardened men.
2. **Sudden wealth is suspicious.**
   She never trusted the narrative around people who "made it" overnight, including my friend John Bosco.
3. **Faith and patience solve problems.**
   She believed hardship was a test, and that God rewarded those who waited faithfully.

These beliefs made my decision difficult to present.

When I entered her room that evening, she was reading her Bible — a nightly ritual she had maintained since I was a child. I waited patiently until she closed it. When I finally told her I wanted to move to Lagos in search of opportunity, she looked at me with concern rather than excitement.

Her first response was simple and expected:

"Lagos is not the answer. If it were easy there, everyone would go."

She had a point. Lagos was not a promised land. It was a grinding machine — one that refined some people and crushed others.

I tried to explain that staying back was no longer an option. I had exhausted every opportunity I could find in the East. For two years, my job search had led to nothing but frustration and silent embarrassment.

Then she asked the question I feared:

"Where will you stay?"

When I mentioned John Bosco, she stiffened. To her, his wealth was not a blessing — it was a warning sign. She had heard the rumors, just like everyone else:

John Bosco is doing 419.
John Bosco's money is not clean.

For many Nigerian parents, such suspicions are enough reason to forbid any association. But suspicion is different when poverty is hovering at your door. When survival is threatened, morality becomes complicated.

I insisted the rumors were exaggerated. She didn't believe me.

Eventually, I did something I am not proud of: I appealed to her fear of shame. I suggested that people would see me as a grown man still depending on his mother, and that she would bear the embarrassment of my failure. It was manipulative, but desperation is a poor advisor. When you feel cornered, you grasp at anything.

Her resistance softened.

She reminded me of a prophecy spoken at my birth — that I would one day lift the family from poverty. Nigerian mothers often hold onto such prophecies as spiritual anchors. To her, preventing me from leaving was equivalent to standing in the way of destiny.

After what felt like a long silence, she gave me her blessing, but with one stern warning:

"If you follow John Bosco into any evil thing, my heart will break."

I assured her I wouldn't. At that moment, I believed my own words — or perhaps I simply needed to believe them.

Within an hour, I had packed my belongings. My younger sister cried openly as I prepared to leave. My mother tried to reassure her with words she didn't fully believe:

"Your brother will bring us money. He will succeed."

They watched me walk out into the dark street toward the night bus station. My mother could not bring herself to escort me. Instead, she stood at the door, whispering prayers under her breath — prayers for protection, for strength, and perhaps for the preservation of the son she feared Lagos might change.

As the bus pulled away, I stared out of the window at the receding lights of my hometown. I felt a mixture of fear, hope, doubt, and determination. I wasn't going to Lagos for adventure. I was going because I was running out of time — and out of dignity.

I didn't know then that the journey ahead would test not just my resilience, but every value I had been raised with. That night, I left home as the person my parents raised.

Lagos would decide who I would become next.

CHAPTER 3 — ARRIVING IN A CITY THAT DEMANDS TRANSFORMATION

The night bus to Lagos was crowded and uncomfortable — the kind of journey Nigerians describe as a test of endurance. People carried their hopes, frustrations, and survival instincts into that bus, and the atmosphere reflected that mix.

The man who sat beside me, a businessman named Donatus, made an impression on me almost immediately. We exchanged pleasantries, but what struck me was the worldview he carried — a worldview shaped by Lagos, a city that forces people to adopt unconventional logic.

At one point, he asked:

"Do you have any madness in your family?"

I thought it was a joke. It wasn't. In Lagos, he explained, "madness" was not insanity — it was the mental toughness required to navigate the city's harshness.

He later unfolded a newspaper, and on the front page was a headline about a British man losing a significant sum of money to a Nigerian scam syndicate. My instinctive response was moral condemnation. His response was the opposite. He described scammers not as criminals, but as "freedom fighters" reclaiming wealth from the West.

His reasoning disturbed me, but it also revealed a truth: **In Nigeria's economic pressure cooker, people develop rationalizations that help them sleep at night.** He had shaped a worldview where fraud was not crime, but "economic justice."

By the time we reached Lagos the next morning, his final words still echoed in my mind:

"This city will change the way you think."

At the time, I dismissed him. But in hindsight, he wasn't warning me — he was predicting me.

When I finally arrived at John Bosco's residence, I realized instantly that this was no ordinary house. It was a walled fortress of wealth — far beyond what any legitimate job could reasonably provide for a 26-year-old.

Lagos had introduced itself in two ways:
On the bus — through ideology.
At the gate of the mansion — through undeniable evidence.

Both messages pointed to the same uncomfortable truth:
The Lagos I had stepped into was built on shadows,

secrets, and moral compromises that few people discussed openly.

And my journey into understanding that world had just begun.

CHAPTER 4 — INSIDE A LIFESTYLE THAT REDEFINES MORAL COMPASS

The first time I walked through John Bosco's house, I felt a combination of awe and disbelief. Everything about the environment projected wealth — not middle-class comfort, but extreme affluence. Imported furniture, high-end electronics, luxury vehicles, and the kind of interior finishing usually reserved for politicians and corporate executives.

Yet, there was no trace of legitimate employment. No office files. No staff going in and out. No evidence of any business. Just wealth — unexplained and abundant.

That contradiction lingered in my mind.

John Bosco had been my childhood friend, someone who grew up under similar circumstances, yet Lagos had transformed him into a figure who now moved with influence. Everywhere we went — upscale restaurants, exclusive lounges, high-end bars — he was treated with respect normally reserved for established businessmen.

That level of attention comes from two things in Lagos: **Money and the belief that more money is coming.**

Over dinners and outings, I began noticing subtle changes in his behavior. He no longer prayed before meals — a small detail, but symbolically significant for someone raised as we were. He spoke about money not as a tool but almost as a religion. The underlying message in everything he said was clear:

"In Lagos, your value is measured in currency, not in character."

He emphasized repeatedly that the job market was essentially a dead end for people like us. He described the city's corporate structure as a hierarchy where nepotism ruled, where connections mattered more than qualifications, and where graduates were exploited as cheap labor.

According to him, 419 was not just an option — it was the only viable path for young men without political or social backing.

I resisted that notion initially. I still believed in the possibility of honest success. But the more time I spent around him — observing the comfort, the influence, the ease with which he navigated spaces — the more the contrast between our realities began to weigh on me.

Lagos was confronting me with a question I could no longer ignore:

Was my moral conviction sustainable in a system designed to reward those who abandoned it?

I didn't answer it then. But the seed of doubt had been planted.

CHAPTER 5 — PRESSURE, POVERTY, AND THE MOMENT THAT BROKE ME

The shift in my life did not happen overnight. It was gradual, shaped by long days of job hunting, silent humiliation, and growing frustration. Lagos did not spare anyone. Every attempt I made to secure employment met the same outcome — rejection or indifference.

Months passed, and I remained dependent on John Bosco's generosity. He never made it seem like a burden, but dependency weighs heavily on any man raised to stand on his own.

Then the breaking point came — not from Lagos itself, but from home.

One afternoon, after returning from another failed interview, I found a letter waiting for me. It was from my younger sister. The contents shook me to the core.

A storm had damaged our home. A roofing sheet had struck my mother, leaving her unconscious for hours. She required immediate surgery. They had no money. They had no home. And she had been asking about me — hoping her son in Lagos was "making progress."

At that moment, sitting in John Bosco's living room with the letter trembling in my hand, I experienced a kind of helplessness I had never known before.

I had no savings.
No job.
No means to assist.
Nothing.

Poverty is not just lack of money. Poverty is psychological violence — the kind that strips away your dignity and your ability to protect the people you love.

John Bosco did not lecture me that day. He simply placed $5,000 in my lap — casually, effortlessly — and said:

"This is what I've been trying to show you. Life doesn't reward conscience. It rewards action."

It was not the money itself that broke me. It was the fact that solving an emergency that could have destroyed my family took him only a few seconds.

I had never touched a foreign currency note before. Now I was holding enough to change my mother's fate — and it didn't come from any job.

I had reached a junction where morality and responsibility collided head-on. And in that moment, **responsibility won**.

Sending the money home required a lie — that I had received a salary advance from a new job. It was the first major lie I ever told my mother. And it marked the beginning of an internal shift I could no longer pretend wasn't happening.

That evening, I made the decision that would alter the course of my life:

"I'm ready. Count me in."

John Bosco reacted with excitement. But for me, it wasn't excitement — it was resignation. A concession that my moral framework had been overwhelmed by circumstances I could no longer control.

That night, as I lay awake staring at the ceiling, I understood what pushes so many young men into the fraud industry.

CHAPTER 6 — CROSSING A LINE I COULD NEVER UNCROSS

The morning after I agreed to join the fraud world, the weight of that decision sat heavily on me. I woke up with a sense of finality — as though a door had closed quietly behind me and another had opened into a world I could no longer deny.

John Bosco walked into my room early and said:

"Today, you begin."

He said it casually, almost cheerfully, but to me it felt like a formal initiation into a life I had spent years condemning.

Before anything began, he reminded me again of the realities that had shaped my choice. The job market in Lagos wasn't just difficult; it was structurally hostile. Companies survived on the cheap labor of desperate graduates. Nepotism governed hiring. Salaries were too small to sustain even basic living expenses in the city.

I had lived that reality for months — long queues, harsh treatment, pointless interviews, empty promises. Lagos forces you to question whether morality is a luxury only the financially secure can afford.

John Bosco's warning echoed a deeper cultural truth:

In Nigeria, poverty is treated like failure — not circumstance.
If you remain poor too long, you become a source of shame.

That morning, I sent money home for my mother's surgery, along with the lie that would become the first of many: a fabricated story about receiving a salary advance from an oil company. I hated that lie, but I justified it as a necessary shield to protect her from the truth.

But what kept me awake that night was the fear of where this road led. Images of arrest, disgrace, and ruin played repeatedly in my mind. Yet, another thought confronted me:

"What other choice do you have?"

By dawn, I understood the reality clearly:
I had stepped out of the world I knew, and I was preparing to enter one governed by different rules — rules enforced not only by people but by belief systems, fear, and secrecy.

When John Bosco said, "Your training starts now," it was not a warning. It was a declaration.

I had crossed the line.
And there was no turning back.

CHAPTER 7 — THE SPIRITUAL ARCHITECTURE OF NIGERIA'S FRAUD UNDERWORLD

Before joining an actual fraud operation, I had assumed scammers simply sat behind laptops, typed deceptive messages, and waited for victims to respond. What I discovered instead was a complex spiritual ecosystem supporting the scam industry — one that blended Christianity, traditional religion, and psychological conditioning in ways I had never imagined.

John Bosco explained this world in two words:

"Spiritual insurance."

In the fraud underworld, success is believed to depend not only on skill, but on spiritual reinforcement. And before I could be accepted as a full participant, I needed to undergo the rituals that shape the mindset, loyalty, and fear that hold the entire network together.

There were two key figures:

1. Prophet Raphael — The Religious Legitimizer

The first stop was a large church operated by a well-known charismatic prophet. I had seen him on television preaching prosperity, divine wealth, and supernatural breakthroughs. What I didn't know was that his ministry quietly catered to high-level fraud syndicates.

I witnessed something that would stay with me for life: A religious space being used not for repentance or healing, but for **empowering deception**.

He prayed over me, invoking "open financial doors" and "divine access to wealth." His language was coded but clear. He reinforced the belief that fraud was blessed, protected, and spiritually sanctioned.

Then came the ritual involving a live ram. Its slaughter and the use of its blood was framed as a cleansing and spiritual exchange — symbolic to believers, coercive to those uncertain, and psychologically binding to recruits.

The intention was clear:
Break down your moral resistance.
Replace guilt with conviction.
Replace hesitation with confidence.
Replace doubt with faith in "destiny."

It was a strategic recalibration of conscience.

2. Doctor Ike — The Enforcer

If the prophet worked on the mind and conscience, the native doctor worked on fear and obedience.

In his shrine, religion did not soften anything. The atmosphere was designed to intimidate.
Bones.
Carvings.
Dark corridors.
And finally — a corpse used in the oath-taking ritual.

Nothing about this ritual was symbolic. It was psychological warfare.

The oath emphasized secrecy, loyalty, and the consequences of betrayal. It was not about belief; it was about deterrence. Once you repeat those words in that environment, something inside you shifts.

John Bosco never asked what happened inside the shrine. No one ever does. Silence is part of the conditioning. The fear of supernatural consequences becomes a tool to ensure loyalty.

A System Rooted in Psychology, Not Just Spirituality

I realized that these rituals serve several purposes:

- **They eliminate guilt.**
- **They create psychological dependence.**
- **They foster loyalty through fear.**
- **They reinforce the idea that leaving the system is impossible.**
- **They elevate fraud from crime to "calling."**

By the time we left the shrine that day, I understood something crucial:

The fraud industry is not held together by money alone, but by belief and fear — two of the most powerful psychological forces on earth.

And now, those forces were shaping me.

CHAPTER 8 — INITIATION: THE DAY I STOPPED BEING WHO I USED TO BE

After the rituals at the church and the shrine, I was physically clean, but mentally disoriented. The experience was overwhelming. I had not simply participated in ceremonies — I had undergone psychological recalibration.

Initiation serves a specific purpose in fraud syndicates: **to erase the old identity and create a new one capable of functioning in the fraud world.**

It wasn't just about spiritual protection. It was about:

- accepting the secrecy
- accepting the hierarchy
- accepting the consequences
- accepting the irreversible nature of the journey

John Bosco referred to this as "dying to your old life."

Why initiation is considered essential

As I reflected on what had happened, it became clear that initiation in the scam industry is not mystical — it is strategic:

1. **It erodes moral resistance.**
   After the rituals, crime feels less like crime.
2. **It instills fear of betrayal.**
   You believe that supernatural punishment awaits anyone who exposes the operation.
3. **It builds a sense of belonging.**
   You feel part of something larger — a network, a brotherhood, a hidden community.
4. **It ensures psychological loyalty even without physical enforcement.**
   Fear controls where security cameras cannot reach.

Returning Home a Different Person

When I got back to the house, I showered repeatedly, but the psychological weight remained. I felt different — not in a mystical sense, but in mindset.

I was no longer a job seeker.
I was no longer an outsider.
I was no longer the person who left home with moral certainty.

I had been initiated — into a world that demands silence, obedience, and a willingness to bend or break the moral code society had taught me.

That night, lying in bed, I understood the truth clearly:

I was inside now.
Not by accident.
Not by coercion.
But by choice forged through desperation, pressure, and survival instinct.

From the next morning onward, it would no longer be about rituals or oaths.
It would be about learning the craft — the operational skills that make the fraud industry function.

The real training was about to begin.

CHAPTER 9 — LEARNING THE RULES OF A HIDDEN ECONOMY

The morning after my initiation, I woke up with a different kind of awareness — not mystical, but psychological. Everything felt unfamiliar, as though I had crossed into a system governed by rules I had not yet fully learned. John Bosco sensed it immediately.

He sat me down and explained the foundational principles that hold the fraud ecosystem together. These were not written laws, yet they controlled everything more strictly than any constitution.

Rule 1: Never Work Alone

Fraud is structured. Every job involves multiple people:

- writers
- callers
- runners
- insiders
- document specialists
- foreign collaborators

No one succeeds as an isolated operator. Lone scammers get caught, confused, or cheated. The ecosystem only functions through collaboration — or at least a version of it.

Rule 2: The Chairman Is Final Authority

Every syndicate has a chairman. He is the strategist, financier, protector, and judge. His decisions are not open for debate.

Chairs maintain:

- relationships with corrupt officers
- access to forged documents
- foreign pipelines
- spiritual backing
- internal discipline

Defying a chairman is not considered an option.

Rule 3: Silence Is Not Just Expected — It Is Enforced

In this world, information is the most valuable commodity. Talking carelessly is the fastest way to end up arrested, expelled, or worse. Silence is taught as survival, not virtue.

Rule 4: Internal Conflict Is Forbidden

A fight between two members is seen as a breach of the entire system. You are not just fighting one person; you are fighting their:

- sponsors
- spiritual backers
- handlers
- allies
- family
- and sometimes their cult affiliations

Conflict threatens the operation. Therefore, leadership crushes it quickly.

Rule 5: Never Get Emotionally Attached to Victims

The industry thrives on detachment. If compassion enters the process, the operation fails. You must see victims not as individuals but as "targets." It is dehumanizing — and deliberately so.

Rule 6: Trust No One Completely

Scammers often scam each other more ruthlessly than they scam foreigners. Paranoia is normalized. Everyone watches everyone. Loyalty is conditional.

Being Exposed to the Underworld's Social Structure

Over the next days, John Bosco took me across Lagos to show me how deeply rooted the scam ecosystem was.

I saw:

- upscale lounges where young men in their twenties spent millions in nights
- private offices disguised as "consultancies" but functioning as fraud command centers
- networks of girlfriends, suppliers, spiritual leaders, and insiders who benefited from the system

I met new faces — some flamboyant, others discreet — all of them operating within the hierarchy.

This was not random crime.
This was an *industry*.

What shocked me most was how normalized everything was. Fraud wasn't whispered about — it was openly celebrated within that circle.

One evening, John Bosco said something that crystallized the entire environment:

"In this business, you rise by understanding people — their fear, greed, loneliness, weakness. If you master that, money will chase you."

He called it "human software engineering."

By the time the chairman asked to meet me, I understood that this world had rules just as rigid as the society outside it — only here, money and silence were the main currencies.

When I stood before the chairman, he asked me a few questions — nothing dramatic. He simply wanted to know whether I was ready to work, obey, and deliver.

His final statement was blunt:

"Once you start, there is no turning back."

He was not threatening me. He was informing me.

And he was right.

CHAPTER 10 — THE ANATOMY OF AN INTERNATIONAL FRAUD NETWORK

Before I could begin operational training, I needed to understand the entire ecosystem — how the fraud machine runs from the inside. Contrary to popular assumptions, internet fraud is not executed by a single person "behind a laptop." It is a sophisticated, distributed network with distinct roles.

John Bosco spent days breaking it down.

1. The Chairman — The Center of Gravity

The chairman does not call victims or touch laptops. He manages:

- funds

- strategy
- internal discipline
- protection
- conflict resolution
- international connections

His influence determines which cases get priority and who gets assigned to high-value jobs.

A chairman is feared not because of violence, but because of:

- his political connections
- his spiritual backing
- his ability to shut down or restart operations

The chairman earns a percentage of every job — a tax on the ecosystem.

---

2. The Writer — The Invisible Architect

Writers craft:

- emotional narratives
- business proposals
- legal documents
- inheritance stories
- NGO appeals
- shipping approvals
- oil and gas contracts

Their skill determines whether victims believe the storyline. Some writers study international law, corporate structures, or logistics to imitate real systems convincingly.

A good writer is invaluable.

---

3. The Caller — The Actor

Callers are performers. They:

- build rapport
- maintain emotional relationships
- control communication
- negotiate
- manipulate
- create urgency

Their voices carry the deception. They often train in accents — American, British, South African, Canadian — depending on the target.

A great caller can milk a victim for months.

---

4. The Insiders — The Hidden Leverage

These are people inside:

- banks
- courier companies
- airports
- telecom companies
- government offices

They provide:

- account verification
- official signatures
- flight documents
- sim card replacements
- international routing information

Without insiders, large scams fail.

---

5. The Runners — The Physical Operators

Runners handle logistics:

- receive parcels
- collect documents
- buy sim cards
- move funds
- transport people
- deliver forged items

They are the connective tissue between digital operations and physical movement.

6. The Forger — The Craftsman

Forgers produce:

- passports
- seals
- certificates
- diplomatic IDs
- bank slips
- customs documents

Their work must withstand scrutiny. Many operate like traditional artisans — quietly, efficiently, and discreetly.

7. International Collaborators — The Global Arm

These partners are deeply embedded in:

- Dubai
- Malaysia
- China
- Turkey
- Europe
- North America

They help:

- cash checks
- run shell companies
- handle crypto
- buy goods
- launder money

419 is global because these collaborators provide the infrastructure.

---

8. Spiritual Backers — The Psychological Reinforcement

Prophets and native doctors maintain the syndicate's emotional stability:

- providing "blessings" for success
- reinforcing loyalty
- invoking fear against betrayal
- reducing guilt
- offering a sense of divine approval

Their influence cannot be overstated.

A Synced, Hidden System

By the time John Bosco finished explaining, it was clear that fraud was not merely financial crime — it was:

- an economic response
- a cultural adaptation
- a psychological system
- a spiritual hybrid
- a survival mechanism

I realized I had entered something far more complex than I ever imagined.

And now, it was time to be trained inside it.

CHAPTER 11 — INSIDE THE TRAINING GROUND

Fraud syndicates in Lagos do not train recruits casually. They operate training centers — referred to as "offices." These are not hidden in slums or abandoned buildings. Many operate inside gated estates, luxury apartments, and commercial complexes disguised as legitimate businesses.

The first office John Bosco took me to looked like a typical Lekki residence from the outside. Inside, it was something entirely different.

A Structured Learning Environment

The office was divided into specialized rooms:

- **Room 1:** NGO scam division
- **Room 2:** Romance and emotional manipulation
- **Room 3:** Oil & Gas (high-value scams)
- **Room 4:** Delivery and diplomatic bag operations

Each room functioned like a department in a corporation. Each room had supervisors, performance targets, and operational rules.

Young men — some barely in their twenties — sat at laptops or paced with phones. Their concentration and discipline resembled that of a professional call center.

Nothing about this looked like "random yahoo yahoo." It was organized crime dressed as structured business.

Observation Before Participation

John Bosco assigned me to follow Nero — a top caller who had mastered multiple accents. Nero treated fraud like an art form. I watched him switch effortlessly between identities, adjust tone to suit different victims, and perform emotional manipulation with practiced ease.

He taught me:

- victims respond to confidence, not sympathy
- urgency triggers action
- paperwork builds credibility
- emotional storytelling builds trust
- pressure amplifies compliance

He summarized it perfectly:

"A mugu must believe the illusion more than the truth."

Understanding the Scale of Money

One of the most shocking experiences was seeing previous job logs. Large sums — tens of thousands, even hundreds of thousands — were recorded like normal business transactions.

For the first time, I saw evidence of:

- global transfers
- cryptocurrency laundering
- corporate-level scams
- gradual victim "milking" strategies

Everything was documented, categorized, and tracked.

It was a full-fledged underground economy.

The Psychological Shift Begins

Training was not just technical. It was designed to:

- reframe guilt
- normalize deception
- reward emotional distance
- reinforce loyalty
- encourage ambition

The more I observed, the more the world outside seemed distant and naive. The logic inside the office felt increasingly normal.

By the time Nero told me:

"Tomorrow, you join the Oil & Gas division,"

I felt something unsettling:

I was ready.

Not because I wanted to deceive anyone,
but because survival had reshaped my priorities.

And because once the system pulls you in,
it slowly convinces you that you belong.

CHAPTER 12 — LEARNING THE SCRIPT: HOW SCAMMERS ARE TRAINED TO THINK AND SPEAK

Before I entered the Oil & Gas division — considered one of the highest-earning arms of the fraud world — I had to master something more important than documents, accents, or digital tricks.

I had to learn **the script**.

Contrary to public assumptions, scammers do not improvise their way through interactions. The industry runs on carefully crafted narratives refined over years of trial, error, and psychological study.

The script is not just a set of words.
The script is *the backbone of the deception.*

The Writer: The Quiet Architect of Fraud

I was paired with Pablo, a highly skilled writer who approached scam scripts the way a lawyer approaches legal briefs. He was calm, analytical, and disturbingly talented.

He showed me folder after folder of templates:

- crude oil allocation contracts
- partnership agreements
- shipping documents
- tax clearance certificates
- diplomatic authorizations
- marine insurance papers

Each document looked professionally designed. Each format mimicked government or corporate paperwork.

To Pablo, these templates weren't "fake documents." They were **props in a psychological performance**.

How the Script Works

Pablo broke the process into phases:

1. The Hook

A short, sharp message that creates curiosity:

- "We urgently require a trusted foreign partner."
- "This proposal is confidential and time-sensitive."

Hooks are designed to stimulate greed or opportunity.

2. The Narrative

A believable backstory — corporate, governmental, or humanitarian — that makes the victim feel chosen.

3. The Drama

The moment of urgency:

- delayed shipments
- bureaucratic obstacles
- last-minute approvals
- security agencies "interfering"

Drama forces decisions.

4. The Payment Stage

The critical phase:

- administrative fees
- storage costs
- clearance payments
- attorney charges

This is where the money comes in.

5. The Ending

Either:

- milking the victim gradually
  or
- taking the final payout and disappearing

The goal is always to maximize extraction without triggering suspicion.

The Psychology Behind Every Line

Pablo emphasized that many victims fail not because they are foolish, but because scripts exploit:

- loneliness
- ambition
- greed
- emotional vulnerability
- trust in official-looking documents

He told me something that echoed throughout my training:

"Humans don't fall for facts. They fall for feelings."

Accent Training

After script mastery came vocal training.
Nero introduced me to Don-Flex, a top caller with remarkable control over tone and accent.

Under his guidance, I practiced:

- British accents for corporate roles
- American accents for legal roles
- South African accents for logistics roles

He made me rehearse lines repeatedly until I could deliver them with authority, even under pressure.

"Your voice must never sound like a request," Don-Flex said.
"It must sound like an instruction."

This was the first time I understood that callers are not liars.
They are performers.

Internal Transformation

As I memorized scripts, practiced accents, and studied victim psychology, something began shifting in me. The script wasn't just teaching me how to deceive others — it was reshaping how I thought, spoke, and saw the world.

The more I trained, the more I detached emotionally.
The more I detached, the easier the deception became.

Pablo saw the change and simply told me:

"Once your conscience stops arguing with the script, you're ready."

He was right.

CHAPTER 13 — FIRST BLOOD: THE CALL THAT CHANGED EVERYTHING

The day of my first real call approached like an exam I could not postpone. Everyone in the office knew it. Nero prepared me. The Master — the most feared and respected caller — supervised me silently.

The pressure was immense. My first victim was an elderly Canadian man named Walter, already partially engaged by the office. My job was to move him from interest to payment.

The moment I dialed his number, my heart pounded so loudly I could hear it in my ears.

He answered after a few rings, his voice weak but polite.

I slipped immediately into my practiced British accent:

"Good afternoon, Mr. Walter. This is Mr. Daniel Green calling regarding your crude allocation file."

He recognized the storyline immediately.
He responded with relief — a sign that the previous emotional groundwork had been effective.

The Call Unfolds

I followed the script:

- reassurance
- authority
- urgency

Everything Pablo had taught me came naturally.

When I mentioned the "administrative clearance fee," Walter hesitated. I panicked internally, but The Master gestured for me to remain calm.

I added controlled urgency, just as Nero instructed:

"We must settle this today, sir, or your file will be suspended."

That line broke his resistance.

Within minutes, he agreed to make the payment.

The Office Reaction

The moment I ended the call, the room erupted:

- applause
- cheers
- praise

Someone shouted:

"Lucas don enter! First blood!"

Nero hugged me.
The Master nodded with quiet approval — a gesture that carried far more weight.

John Bosco clapped my back proudly.

But the victory didn't feel like celebration to me.
Not at first.

Later that evening, when I was alone, the reality hit me:

I had deceived an elderly man.
He trusted me.
He believed me.
He depended on my voice and my instructions.

And I had used that trust against him.

The Psychological Turning Point

The guilt was sharp — but short-lived.

Another thought drowned it out:

This is how you will feed your family.
This is how you will survive Lagos.
This is how you will escape poverty.

Survival has a way of silencing conscience.

When Walter's payment arrived the next morning, the office celebrated again. I received my share. I saw real money enter my account for the first time.

John Bosco looked at me and said:

"Now you see why nobody goes back."

He was right.
The fraud world had a new operator.
And I was becoming part of the machine.

CHAPTER 14 — BECOMING THE CALLER

After my first successful job, my place in the office changed. I was no longer the new recruit being "tested." I was now an operational caller — and with that came a new level of confidence.

Not confidence in fraud.
Confidence in **my voice**, **my control**, **my ability to influence**.

People in the office began to treat me differently.
They saw potential — someone who could climb far in the hierarchy.

The Goblin Within

There is a concept scammers refer to informally as "the goblin" — the part of you that enjoys the chase, the manipulation, the role-playing, the psychological victory.

At first, I thought it was just office slang.
Then I began to feel it.

It is not evil.
It is not madness.
It is something more subtle:

a shift in your moral center of gravity.

As the calls increased:

- guilt faded
- doubt lessened
- confidence grew
- empathy dulled

I could feel my mind adjusting to the environment's logic.

Improvement Through Experience

Nero intensified my training:

- how to control silence on a call

- how to use background sounds for credibility
- how to adjust tone based on the victim's age
- how to escalate urgency without sounding desperate
- how to defuse suspicion

Each day, I improved.

One of the calls that solidified my confidence was with a German businessman, a difficult target known to challenge details. Yet, when he tried to intimidate me, I found myself responding with controlled authority:

"Mr. Schmidt, if you continue in this manner, I will have no choice but to suspend your file."

He immediately softened.

That was the moment I realized I was no longer pretending.
I was operating.

Identity Reconstruction

The fraud system had reshaped me:

- from a job seeker to a strategist
- from a desperate graduate to a confident operator
- from a moral thinker to a pragmatic manipulator

The transformation was not sudden.
It was gradual, reinforced by:

- money
- praise
- results
- the illusion of power
- the sense of belonging

Every successful call strengthened the new identity forming inside me.

A New Role in the Ecosystem

By the end of that week, the chairman had taken note of my performance. I was now officially part of the Oil & Gas division — a department reserved for the most skilled and profitable operators.

I was rising.
Rapidly.

And with each rise, the possibility of turning back became smaller.

CHAPTER 15 — THE SCAM WITHIN THE SCAMMERS

One of the most surprising realities I encountered inside the fraud underworld was this simple truth:

Scammers scam each other.

Not occasionally.
Not by mistake.
But as a normal part of the ecosystem.

People often imagine the scam world as a united front of criminals working together against foreign victims. In reality, it is a competitive, ego-driven, high-pressure environment where deceit becomes second nature — even among colleagues.

Nero, my mentor, warned me early:

"Every scammer has another scammer living inside him. Watch your back."

At first, I didn't fully understand what he meant. But as I remained in the system, I saw it clearly.

Fraud is not merely an occupation — it is a psychological environment.
And in that environment, betrayal becomes as common as breathing.

---

1. Stealing Victims: The Most Common Internal Crime

If a caller discovers a promising victim — someone emotional, wealthy, or vulnerable — that victim becomes an asset. Other operators monitor this carefully.

Some will:

- hack into the caller's email
- listen in on calls
- copy scripts
- redirect communication
- call the victim pretending to be a superior officer

Once the victim begins responding to the new caller, the original operator is cut off.

The goal is simple:
take over the victim before the victim pays.

Nero once told me:

"A big mugu is like gold. People will kill for gold."

It wasn't a metaphor.
It was reality.

---

2. The Vanishing Colleague

Sometimes, after a successful cash-out, one operator —
especially the one in charge of receiving funds —
disappears.

Completely.

Phone switched off.
Location unknown.
Social media deleted.
SIM cards destroyed.
House vacated.

In some cases, the person relocates to another state.
In others, they flee the country.
In a few, their disappearance remains a mystery forever.

And the chairman rarely investigates.
Why?

Because betrayal is considered a cost of doing business.

---

3. Document Manipulation and Data Theft

Writers are also vulnerable.
They craft documents that callers depend on, but some writers secretly sell premium templates to multiple offices. This causes:

- identical scripts
- duplicated stories
- victims comparing emails
- collapse of major operations

But the writers do it anyway — because each sale brings more money.

---

4. Spiritual Backstabbing

In the fraud world, spirituality is not only used to enforce loyalty; it is also weaponized internally.

Some operators:

- visit native doctors secretly
- request charms to weaken a colleague
- perform rituals to claim the victim of another team

- ask for "open road" spells that shut down others' jobs

Inside this world, even prayers become competitive.

The Psychology Behind the Betrayals

Fraud reshapes the mind.
It amplifies:

- impatience
- entitlement
- ego
- paranoia
- greed

And once you begin to believe that money is the only measure of success, then loyalty becomes an obstacle, not a value.

Nero explained it calmly one night:

"This business changes your brain. Even your friends become competitors. You will learn."

He was right.

Inside the fraud industry, the real danger isn't always the police.
Sometimes, it's the person sitting next to you.

CHAPTER 16 — LAW ENFORCEMENT, SURVEILLANCE, AND THE CONSTANT THREAT OF CAPTURE

As I rose within the network, I began to understand another fundamental truth:

The fraud world is under constant surveillance — but rarely in the way outsiders imagine.

Movies portray dramatic raids, high-speed chases, and sophisticated busts. Reality is different. Law enforcement in Nigeria, and globally, approaches fraud in ways shaped by politics, bureaucracy, and economics — not just morality.

1. EFCC: The Most Visible Threat

The Economic and Financial Crimes Commission (EFCC) is the agency Nigerians fear most in relation to fraud. They conduct:

- periodic raids
- hotel sweeps
- random checkpoint arrests
- public parades of suspects

But here's the truth insiders know:

EFCC is more focused on **visible enforcement** than on dismantling entire networks.

Why?

Because the real networks have:

- political protection
- bank insiders
- powerful sponsors
- spiritual coverage
- international partnerships

EFCC arrests the accessible, not the protected.

In the office, we constantly monitored EFCC activity. Insiders within the agency leaked information.

Someone would announce:

"EFCC is operating in Lekki Phase 1 today."

And operations would pause immediately.

---

2. The Police: A Negotiable Threat

Regular police officers were seldom feared.

Their role in the fraud ecosystem was largely:

- extortion
- bribery
- occasional intimidation

Arrests at checkpoints were common, but almost always resolved with money.

A policeman who sees a young man in an expensive car rarely thinks of morality.
He thinks of "settlement."

---

3. Interpol and Foreign Security Agencies

These were the real threats for high-level operators.

Callers were trained to identify:

- American FBI patterns
- Canadian anti-fraud tactics
- European cybercrime surveillance
- Asian financial reporting systems

Some victims, especially from Europe, contact their local police early. That begins a trail:

- bank traces
- email server checks
- IP monitoring
- diplomatic inquiries

But foreign agencies struggle because:

- victims delay reporting
- fraud networks constantly move
- forgers operate offline
- multiple SIM cards prevent tracking
- compromised officials leak information

Despite global surveillance, most large syndicates remain untouched.

---

4. The Internal Intelligence System

Every fraud office has its own intelligence network. Insiders in:

- telecom companies
- banks
- courier firms
- police stations
- embassies

provide information ahead of law enforcement actions.

This is why fraud networks survive.

They are not just criminals.
They are connected.

---

5. The Fear Every Operator Carries

As confident as we became, there was always a silent fear:

- the fear of a raid
- the fear of an informant
- the fear of a careless colleague
- the fear of an international trace

Some nights, I woke up sweating, imagining the sound of a loud knock on the door.

In this world, **fear becomes part of your daily operating system**.

Even the chairman once said:

"If you don't fear anything, then something is wrong. Fear keeps you sharp."

He was right.

Fraud may pay, but it never feels safe.

CHAPTER 17 — WHAT THE WORLD GETS WRONG ABOUT 419

One of the most important parts of my journey — and ultimately the reason for telling my story — is correcting the misconceptions about Nigeria's fraud world.

The global narrative is simple: **"Nigerian scammers are greedy criminals."**

But the truth is far more complex, layered, and uncomfortable.

---

1. 419 Is Not Driven Only by Greed — It Is Driven by Desperation

Most young men who enter fraud do not wake up one day and choose crime.
They are shaped by:

- unemployment
- poverty
- poor governance
- lack of opportunities
- family pressure
- failed education systems
- widening inequality

Desperation is a powerful motivator.

---

2. Fraud Is Not a Random Hustle — It Is a Structured Industry

419 is:

- organized
- hierarchical
- global
- collaborative
- technologically advanced
- spiritually reinforced

It resembles a corporation more than a street crime.

---

3. Not All Victims Are Innocent

This is difficult to state, but true.

Some victims approach scammers because:

- they believe they are participating in illegal business deals
- they think they're helping move "stolen oil"
- they want a share of "frozen funds"
- they want cheap commodities through unofficial channels

Scammers exploit greed as much as vulnerability.

---

4. Fraud Survives Because Systems Fail

Fraud thrives where:

- jobs are scarce
- institutions are weak
- corruption is widespread
- economic inequality is extreme
- young people lack alternatives

419 is not just a criminal industry — it is a **social symptom**.

---

5. The Media Shows Symptoms, Not Causes

Most documentaries highlight:

- loud lifestyles
- police raids
- flashy cars

But they rarely address:

- systemic unemployment
- poor governance
- economic frustration
- the allure of fast wealth
- spiritual manipulation
- psychological conditioning

You cannot eradicate fraud without addressing *why* it exists.

---

6. The World Underestimates the Intelligence Within the System

Many assume scammers are uneducated or foolish.
Yet some of the smartest people I ever met were inside that world:

- writers who could mimic legal documents flawlessly
- callers who understood human psychology deeply
- forgers who produced near-perfect replicas
- strategists who mapped entire international operations

What society calls "intelligence," fraud calls "skill."

---

7. The System Pulls You In Slowly — And Refuses to Let Go

Fraud reshapes your:

- thinking
- values
- perception of money
- fear
- ambition
- identity

Once you rise inside the system, leaving becomes difficult — not because of threats, but because of the **lifestyle**, the **money**, and the **momentum**.

A Reality the World Must Understand

419 is not just a Nigerian crime.
It is a Nigerian story — one born out of:

- corrupted systems
- broken dreams
- spiritual manipulation
- socio-economic frustration
- and global inequality

If you want to understand Nigerian fraud, you must understand Nigeria.

Because **419 is not merely a crime — it is a mirror reflecting the society that produced it.**

CHAPTER 18 — HITTING THE WALL: WHEN THE MONEY CAN NO LONGER NUMB YOU

Every scammer eventually reaches a point the industry politely avoids talking about — a psychological wall.

It is the moment when:

- the money stops thrilling you
- the calls no longer excite you
- the lies begin to feel repetitive
- the lifestyle starts to feel hollow
- and the fear becomes heavier than the profit

For some, this wall comes after years.
For others, it appears suddenly.

For me, it arrived quietly — not through a raid, not through a betrayal, not through spiritual fear — but through exhaustion.

1. When Every Day Looks the Same

At first, the fraud world feels like a fast-moving train:

- the money grows
- your influence expands
- the praise increases
- your confidence escalates

But once you reach a certain level, you notice something uncomfortable:

Nothing new is happening.
It is the same script, the same lies, the same calls, the same hustle — just with bigger numbers.

Success becomes routine.
Routine becomes boredom.
Boredom becomes introspection.

And introspection is dangerous in an industry that thrives on emotional numbness.

---

2. A Call That Broke Through My Armor

The moment that shook me wasn't dramatic.
It wasn't a major job.
It wasn't a large payout.

It was a simple call with a woman named Mrs. Harding — an elderly widow from the UK. She was kind, trusting, and lonely. She told me she had no children. She said I reminded her of her late husband because of my "gentle voice."

The guilt I had buried resurfaced for the first time in months.

When she said,

"I hope I'm not being foolish trusting you," something in me cracked.

I brushed it off, finished the call, and passed her along the operational chain. But the words stayed with me.

Fraud requires a certain psychological distance.
But in that moment, the distance vanished.

---

3. The Isolation No One Talks About

People assume scammers are surrounded by friends, girls, and joy. The truth is more complex.

The higher you rise:

- the fewer real friends you have
- the more paranoid you become
- the more isolated you feel

- the more people around you expect something from you

You stop trusting.
You stop relaxing.
You stop being yourself.

You become a performance.
A persona.
A voice.

Not a person.

---

4. When the Lifestyle Turns Burdensome

Luxury loses its shine quickly when it becomes routine.

Clubs that once excited you start to feel loud.
Champagne bottles begin to taste the same.
People praising you start sounding insincere.
Women chasing you for money start to feel transactional.

Everywhere you turn, life feels crowded yet strangely empty.

John Bosco once joked:

"The problem with fraud money is that it feeds your body but starves your soul."

At the time, I dismissed it.
Now, I understood it.

---

5. Quiet Doubts Become Loud Questions

I began asking myself:

- *How long can this continue?*
- *What happens if I fall sick?*
- *What happens if someone betrays the office?*
- *What happens if a victim reports early and foreign agents trace it?*
- *What happens if I simply lose my nerve one day?*

Questions like these don't appear early in your fraud career.
They come when you have tasted enough money to see what it can't fix.

And the truth hit me:

This was not a life.
This was a cycle.

A cycle designed to consume you.

CHAPTER 19 — ESCAPING WITHOUT LEAVING: THE GRAY ZONE BETWEEN FRAUD AND FREEDOM

Leaving the fraud world is one of the hardest decisions an operator can make.
Not because the system physically traps you — but because it psychologically binds you.

You don't walk away from fraud the way you resign from a job.
You drift away gradually, silently, strategically.

The fraud world doesn't punish people for leaving.
It punishes people for leaving noisily.

So I entered the **gray zone** — the space between active involvement and quiet withdrawal.

---

1. Reducing Calls Slowly

The first step was subtle.
I reduced my hours.
I took fewer cases.
I avoided high-value targets.
I allowed other callers to take lead roles.

No one questioned it.
When a top performer slows down, people assume he's working "privately" or handling an independent foreign client.

In fraud, privacy is normal.
And assumptions protect you.

---

2. Increasing Absences Without Explanation

I began disappearing for days at a time:

- staying at home
- visiting family
- traveling internally

- focusing on personal development

People thought I was managing a large job privately.
No one asked questions.

Fraud offices respect privacy the way corporations
respect seniority.

---

3. Cleaning My Digital Footprint

I gradually:

- deleted email accounts
- wiped devices
- removed old scripts
- destroyed SIM cards
- backed up nothing

I left nothing that could be traced.

In this world, people get comfortable.
They save evidence.
They believe they are invincible.

I knew better.

---

4. Redirecting My Money and Mind

I invested quietly:

- small businesses
- family support
- personal projects

I spent less.
I showed less.
I appeared less.

The lifestyle slowed down.

And strangely, I felt… lighter.

---

5. Accepting That Leaving Is Not One Big Decision

People think leaving fraud is a dramatic moment — an epiphany, a spiritual awakening, a life-threatening experience.

It rarely happens like that.

Leaving fraud is:

- a slow internal shift
- a gradual withdrawal

- a quiet reawakening
- a recognition of fatigue
- a desire for peace

And most importantly:

a realization that the money is not worth the mental weight anymore.

I wasn't out yet.
But I was no longer fully in.

I was in the gray zone — the most dangerous but necessary stage.

CHAPTER 20 — CLOSING THE DOOR WITHOUT MAKING NOISE

Leaving the fraud world entirely required a final decision — one that demanded calmness, not emotion.

People leave fraud in three typical ways:

1. **Arrest** — the system forces you out.
2. **Burnout** — your mind collapses before your body.
3. **Awakening** — you quietly choose a different path.

I belonged to the third group.

---

1. Understanding the Cost of Staying

By the time I reached the end of my fraud journey, I had seen:

- arrests
- betrayals
- spiritual breakdowns
- mental collapse
- paranoia

- operators losing loved ones
- people disappearing

Fraud offers money.
But the cost is your peace.

And peace is priceless.

---

2. The Gentle Exit

I didn't announce my departure.
I didn't confess to colleagues.
I didn't burn bridges.

I simply reduced involvement until my absence became normal.

Eventually, invitations stopped.
Calls reduced.
People moved on to new recruits, new victims, new operations.

The fraud world does not mourn absences.
It replaces them.

---

3. Rebuilding Myself Quietly

I began:

- studying
- rebuilding my faith
- reconnecting with family
- investing in legitimate ventures
- mentoring younger relatives
- re-entering society slowly

I became a different person — not instantly, not perfectly — but gradually.

Healing is slow.
Transformation is slower.
But progress is possible.

---

4. The Truth About Leaving Fraud

Leaving fraud does not make you holy.
It does not erase your past.
It does not remove the memories.
It does not remove the guilt.

But it gives you something far more important:

Clarity.
Peace.
Identity.
Direction.

Fraud is a world that consumes identity.
Leaving allows you to reclaim it.

5. Why I Chose to Tell This Story

This book is not written to:

- glamorize fraud
- shame victims
- condemn operators
- justify crime

It is written to:

- document truth
- explain the internal machinery
- show the psychological toll
- provide insight from someone who lived it
- prevent others from falling into the same trap

My journey is real.
My mistakes are real.
My transformation is real.

If this story keeps one young person from being lured into fraud — the book has done its job.

CHAPTER 21 — THE COST OF SILENCE

One of the hardest realizations after stepping away from the fraud world is understanding that silence has a cost. When you leave, the world does not welcome you back with applause. There are no "congratulations." There is no ceremony. There is no rehabilitation center for ex-scammers. You simply become another person trying to rebuild a life from the shadows.

People often believe that leaving crime is the victory. But the real struggle begins *after* you leave.

1. Living with Secrets

For a long time, I couldn't talk about where I had been or what I had done. Society punishes honesty in these matters. Even people who appear understanding often carry judgment behind their smiles.

I quickly learned:

- what to say
- what to avoid
- what to hide
- what to reframe
- what to bury

Silence protects you, but it also isolates you.

There were nights I lay awake replaying the voices of victims, the pressure of the office, the rituals, the danger, the mistakes, the close calls. These memories don't vanish. They linger.

Leaving the fraud world does not erase the past.
It only forces you to confront it quietly.

---

2. The Psychological Aftermath

Fraud reshapes the mind in ways that take time to undo:

- You become overly cautious.
- You anticipate betrayal.
- You read too much into people's motives.
- You second-guess every relationship.
- You struggle to trust.

Healing requires:

- patience
- self-awareness
- humility
- forgiveness of self
- spiritual grounding

And none of these come instantly.

---

3. Watching Others Fall

After leaving, I watched many colleagues continue down the same road. Some were arrested. Some ran mad. Some died suddenly. Some vanished without explanation.

A few tried to leave but were pulled back by the lure of fast money.

The fraud world has a gravitational pull — it draws people back in when their finances drop or life pressures hit.

Seeing others fall reminded me why leaving had been necessary.

---

4. Facing the Person in the Mirror

The hardest part of leaving fraud is not escaping the system.
It is learning to live with yourself again.

For years, I had been performing roles:

- caller
- manipulator
- strategist
- actor
- deceiver

Now I had to remember who I was before the fraud world reconstructed me.

That process was painful.
But it was the first step toward regaining control of my own identity.

CHAPTER 22 — REBUILDING FROM THE GROUND UP

Rebuilding after fraud is not as simple as starting a new life. Fraud gives you money, but it takes away stability, peace, trust, and structure. When you walk away, you start with none of those things.

You begin from zero — emotionally, financially, socially, and spiritually.

---

1. The Slow Return to Legitimacy

Legitimate income felt strange at first.
The pace was slow.
The earnings were small.
The work required discipline and patience — two skills the fraud world hardly encourages.

In the scam world, money comes in waves.
In legitimate life, money comes in drops.

Adjusting to "drops" was a humbling experience.

---

2. Relearning Discipline

Fraud rewards:

- improvisation
- boldness
- speed
- manipulation

Real life rewards:

- consistency
- patience
- humility
- long-term planning

I had to relearn:

- waking up early
- setting daily goals
- managing expenses
- building sustainable income
- thinking long-term

These skills were rusty, but not lost.

---

3. Reconnecting with Family Without Guilt

One of the most painful parts of leaving fraud is returning to family without the financial power you once had.
Fraud gives you the ability to solve problems quickly.
Legitimate life slows that ability down.

Explaining this shift is almost impossible.
People see the reduction in financial flow and assume:

- mismanagement
- irresponsibility
- bad luck

But I kept silent.
Not out of shame — but because truth can sometimes cause more damage than healing.

Instead, I gradually re-established myself:

- supporting where I could
- being present consistently
- repairing relationships
- showing genuine change

Real responsibility is not measured by the amount you give, but by the consistency with which you show up.

4. Returning to Faith

Fraud distorts spirituality.
It introduces compromise, fear, and superstition.
When you leave, you must unlearn all of that.

My return to faith was not dramatic.
It was quiet:

- private prayers
- honest reflections
- slow forgiveness of myself
- rebuilding trust in God
- releasing fear of spiritual retaliation

You cannot rebuild outwardly if you are broken
inwardly.

CHAPTER 23 — THE REASON THIS STORY MUST BE TOLD

The greatest misconception about leaving the fraud world is that redemption begins when you step out. In truth, redemption begins only when you speak out — not to confess crime, but to illuminate the path others are blindly walking toward.

This book exists because silence helps no one.

---

1. Young People Need to Hear the Truth

Nigerian youth are being lured into fraud at an alarming rate:

- through social media
- through flashy influencers
- through pressure from families
- through economic hardship
- through desperation

No one tells them the whole story.

They see:

- the cars
- the clothes

- the parties
- the attention
- the lifestyle

But they never see:

- the fear
- the emptiness
- the mental stress
- the betrayals
- the spiritual confusion
- the loneliness
- the paranoia
- the traps

Someone must say it plainly:

Fraud does not free you.
It captures you.
Quietly. Gradually. Completely.

---

2. Society Must Understand the Causes

419 is not just a criminal problem.
It is a socioeconomic and psychological crisis.

Unless Nigeria addresses:

- unemployment
- failed education

- corruption
- broken systems
- lack of opportunities
- spiritual exploitation

fraud will continue.

---

3. Victims Need a Human Explanation

Victims often wonder:

- "Why did this happen to me?"
- "How could someone deceive me like this?"

Understanding the psychology behind fraud allows them to heal without blaming themselves unnecessarily.

Scammers exploit:

- loneliness
- greed
- curiosity
- vulnerability
- trust

It is not always stupidity.
It is human nature.

---

4. Former Operators Need a Pathway Out

This book is also for those still inside the fraud world —
the ones who feel trapped but don't know how to leave.

Leaving is possible.
Healing is possible.
Rebuilding is possible.
Transformation is possible.

But someone must show the steps.
Someone must speak from inside.
Someone must break the silence.

The Purpose

This story is not about glorification.
It is not about justification.
It is not about condemnation.

It is about **truth**.

A truth that can:

- educate
- warn
- guide
- prevent
- rehabilitate

- inspire change

This is why I chose to tell it.
To shine light where young people often walk blindly.
To expose a system many misunderstand.
To show that redemption is real — even after choices you regret.

CONCLUSION — THE ROAD BACK TO MYSELF

When I look back on the years I spent inside the fraud world, I see a young man shaped not by greed or wickedness, but by desperation, pressure, and a system that failed to protect his dignity. I see someone who entered Lagos with hope, was swallowed by its realities, and eventually had to claw his way back to sanity.

This story is not an excuse.
It is an examination.
It is not a justification.
It is a confession.
It is not a glorification.
It is a warning.

I have lived on both sides of morality — the side that society praises, and the side it fears. I understand how easily a good person can cross into darkness when surrounded by the wrong environment and the wrong pressures. I understand how crime is not always born from evil, but from survival. And I understand how leaving that world requires courage, patience, and deep honesty.

Fraud changes you.
Leaving fraud changes you even more.

---

1. The Real Victory Is Not Money — It Is Clarity

There was a time when I believed success was measured by the weight of your pocket or the sound of respect in other people's voices. But life eventually teaches you that true success is internal:

- peace of mind
- self-respect
- emotional stability
- the ability to look in the mirror with honesty

Money can buy distractions.
It cannot buy peace.

When I walked away from the fraud world, I didn't walk into wealth.
I walked into clarity — and clarity is priceless.

---

2. Healing Is Not a Moment — It Is a Journey

I did not wake up one day free from guilt, from fear, or from the memories of the people I deceived. Healing was slow:

- reconciling with faith
- forgiving myself
- rebuilding relationships
- returning to purpose
- rediscovering identity

Healing required admitting that I had been both a victim and a participant — shaped by circumstances, yet responsible for my choices.

Healing required humility.

---

3. A Generation Is Crying Out — And No One Is Listening

Nigeria is filled with young people who feel trapped between two roads:

- the road of honest suffering
- the road of dishonest survival

Both roads are broken.

Until we fix:

- unemployment
- corruption
- failed systems
- inequality
- broken education
- lack of opportunity

fraud will continue to rise.

Young people are not turning to crime because they enjoy it.
They are turning because society has closed every legitimate door.

We cannot fight fraud without fighting the conditions that create it.

---

4. Redemption Must Be Possible — Even for Those Who Strayed

Former fraud operators rarely talk because:

- society judges
- the law threatens
- families don't understand

- the system offers no rehabilitation

But redemption cannot be reserved only for those who made socially acceptable mistakes.
It must also extend to those who lost their way in dark places but found the courage to return.

If we cannot forgive people who made wrong turns under pressure, then we cannot claim to be building a compassionate society.

---

5. Why This Story Matters

This book exists for three groups of people:

For the youth standing on the edge

To show them the full truth — not the flashy lies.
To show them that fraud is a cage, not a shortcut.
To warn them before they make a mistake they may not escape.

For the society that judges without understanding

To demonstrate that behind every "scammer" is:

- a story
- a family

- a wound
- a system
- and a series of events that shaped their path

Understanding does not mean condoning.
It means responding wisely.

For the people still trapped inside the fraud world

To tell them that leaving is possible.
That life exists outside the fear and the pressure.
That peace is real.
That purpose can be rebuilt.
That identity can be reclaimed.

My Hope Moving Forward

As I close this chapter of my life and share it with the world, my hope is that this book becomes:

- a mirror
- a warning
- a lesson
- and a guide

I hope it inspires:

- empathy

- reform
- awareness
- dialogue
- and change

Not just for Nigeria — but for any society where young people are forced to choose between integrity and survival.

In the end, this book is not about crime.
It is about humanity — flawed, pressured, resilient humanity.
It is about the difficult paths we walk, the mistakes we make, and the possibility of becoming better in spite of them.

And it is about me — a man who entered the darkness, confronted himself, and found his way back into the light.

Not perfectly.
Not instantly.
But honestly.

This is my story.
And this is my truth.

ACKNOWLEDGEMENTS

This book is not the story of one man alone. It is the product of many people, experiences, and lessons woven into a journey that shaped me deeply.

First, I acknowledge **God**, whose grace preserved me in moments when I did not even understand I needed preservation. Walking away from the fraud world was not just strength — it was mercy.

To my **mother**, whose quiet prayers followed me everywhere. Your faith was the foundation I returned to, even when I drifted into darkness. Your resilience inspired my conscience, and your love reminded me of the man I was raised to be.

To my **family**, thank you for your patience, support, and belief in my transformation. Healing is easier when you are surrounded by people who want to see you rise.

To the **friends who stayed**, who understood my silence without demanding explanation — thank you. The world judges loudly; genuine friends understand quietly.

To the **victims impacted by the fraud ecosystem**, whether directly or indirectly, this book is also for you. May these insights offer clarity, help you heal, and remind you that your trust was misused, not your intelligence.

To the **youth reading this**, searching for purpose in a difficult world — may this story guide you, warn you, and give you the courage to walk the right path, even when it feels slow.

And finally, to those who will use this book for research, education, policy work, or rehabilitation — thank you for caring enough to understand the human story behind the headlines.

GLOSSARY OF TERMS

419

A popular Nigerian slang for internet fraud, named after Section 419 of the Nigerian Criminal Code dealing with fraudulent activities.

Chairman

The leader of a fraud syndicate. Oversees operations, finances, protection, and decision-making.

Caller

Operator who communicates directly with victims, using scripts, accents, manipulation, and psychological tactics.

Writer

Specialist who creates scripts, fake documents, narratives, email templates, and storylines used in fraud operations.

Mugu

Scammer slang for a victim. Also referred to as "client" or "fish."

Oil & Gas Format

A high-level scam involving fake crude allocations, contracts, and shipping documents designed to target wealthy individuals or companies.

Delivery Format

A scam involving fake parcels, diplomatic bags, customs clearance fees, or shipping delays.

Romance Format

Fraud based on emotional manipulation, often involving fake identities and long-term trust-building.

Native Doctor (Baba)

A traditional spiritual practitioner consulted for rituals, charms, or oaths used to reinforce loyalty or protection in the fraud world.

Prophet

A religious figure used by syndicates for prayers, "spiritual backing," or psychological reinforcement.

Office

A fraud training or operational center disguised as a legitimate business or apartment.

Ritual/Oath

Spiritual ceremony conducted to ensure secrecy, loyalty, and fear-based obedience within a syndicate.

Runner

A person who handles physical logistics such as receiving parcels, collecting SIM cards, or delivering forged documents.

Format

The specific fraud method or storyline being used in an operation (e.g., NGO format, oil format, romance format).

Cash Out

The moment money is successfully collected from a victim.

Tight

Industry slang for a victim who is convinced and ready to pay.

APPENDIX A: PSYCHOLOGY OF INTERNET FRAUD

This appendix summarizes the psychological mechanisms scammers use to influence victims, based on patterns observed during my time in the industry.

1. Authority Bias

Scammers project official titles or legal language to appear credible.

2. Urgency and Time Pressure

Deadlines force victims to make decisions quickly without verification.

3. Emotional Mirroring

Scammers reflect victims' emotions, creating false rapport.

4. Greed and Reward Anticipation

Some victims respond to opportunities for quick profit.

5. Fear and Threat

Subtle warnings are used to push victims into compliance.

6. Loneliness and Connection

Especially common in romance scams; emotional vulnerability is exploited.

APPENDIX B: WHY YOUTHS ENTER THE FRAUD WORLD

A summary of socio-economic factors driving 419:

1. Unemployment Crisis

Nigeria's job market is unable to absorb millions of young graduates yearly.

2. Inequality and Social Pressure

Society expects financial success early, often without providing legitimate pathways.

3. Failed Systems

Education, governance, and economic structures push many toward desperate choices.

4. The Illusion of Fast Wealth

Social media glorifies success without showing the cost or consequences.

5. Lack of Awareness

Few youths understand how destructive fraud is — especially mentally and spiritually.

APPENDIX C: HOW VICTIMS CAN PROTECT THEMSELVES

1. Verify All Unsolicited Emails

Especially those involving money, contracts, or inheritance.

2. Avoid Sending Money to Unknown Parties

No legitimate institution requests personal payments through unofficial channels.

3. Be Suspicious of "Too Good to Be True" Offers

Especially involving oil contracts, diplomatic shipments, or emergency fees.

4. Seek Legal Advice

Before signing or sending any document, consult a lawyer.

5. Trust Your Instincts

If something feels off, it likely is.

ABOUT THE AUTHOR

Frederick Amakom is a Nigerian writer, researcher, and commentator with a passion for social issues, youth development, and the hidden structures shaping modern African society. Born and raised in South Eastern Nigeria, he experienced firsthand the pressures, economic challenges, and cultural expectations that often push young people toward dangerous paths.

After leaving the fraud world and rebuilding his life, Frederick dedicated himself to education, storytelling, and advocacy. His work focuses on revealing the human truths behind social problems — not to justify wrongdoing, but to illuminate the conditions, psychology, and systems that create them. His writing blends lived experience with sober analysis, offering readers an unfiltered look into worlds often misunderstood.

His mission is simple:
to tell the truth, educate the youth, and inspire change.

www.ingramcontent.com/pod-product-compliance
Lightning Source LLC
Chambersburg PA
CBHW051055050326

40690CB00006B/733